D0928011

Vanessa Hudgens

By Valerie Sherrard

Crabtree Publishing Company

www.crabtreebooks.com

Crabtree Publishing Company
www.crabtreebooks.com

Author: Valerie Sherrard
Publishing plan research and development:
Sean Charlebois, Reagan Miller
Crabtree Publishing Company
Project coordinator: Kathy Middleton
Photo research: Crystal Sikkens
Editor: Molly Aloian
Proofreader and Indexer: Wendy Scavuzzo
Designer: Ken Wright
Production coordinator and Prepress technician: Ken Wright

Photographs:
Alamy: © Moviestore Collection Ltd.: pages 12–13
Associated Press: page 18
BigStockPhoto: page 19
Getty Images: © Gary Gershoff/WireImage: page 8; © Bruce Glikas/FilmMagic: page 10
Keystone Press: © Rena Durham/Zuma KPA: page 4; © Mavrixphoto.com: page 6; © Summit Entertainment/zumapress: page 7; © FAME Pictures: pages 9, 21; © Michel Boutefeu: page 11; © Russ Elliot/AdMedia: page 15; © Felipe Trueba/UPPA/Zuma: page 16; © FOTOS International: page 17; © Summit Entertainment: page 22; © Sony Pictures: page 23; © VPC/wenn.com: page 24; © Paul Smith/Featureflash: pages 25, 26; © Jason Mitchell/BuzzFoto.com: page 27
Photoshot: cover
Shutterstock: pages 1, 5, 20, 28

Every effort has been made to trace copyright holders and to obtain their permission for use of copyright material. The authors and publishers would be pleased to rectify any error or omission in future editions. All the Internet addresses given in this book were correct at the time of going to press. The author and publishers regret any inconvenience caused if addresses have changed or sites have ceased to exist, but can accept no responsibility for any such changes.

Library and Archives Canada Cataloguing in Publication

Sherrard, Valerie
Vanessa Hudgens / Valerie Sherrard.

(Superstars!)
Includes index.
Issued also in an electronic format.
ISBN 978-0-7787-7253-8 (bound).--ISBN 978-0-7787-7262-0 (pbk.)

1. Hudgens, Vanessa, 1988- --Juvenile literature.
2. Actors--United States--Biography--Juvenile literature.
3. Singers--United States--Biography--Juvenile literature.
I. Title. II. Series: Superstars! (St. Catharines, Ont.)

PN2287.H83S54 2011   j791.4302'8092   C2010-905309-5

Library of Congress Cataloging-in-Publication Data

Sherrard, Valerie.
Vanessa Hudgens / by Valerie Sherrard.
p. cm. -- (Superstars!)
Includes index.
ISBN 978-0-7787-7262-0 (pbk. : alk. paper) --
ISBN 978-0-7787-7253-8 (reinforced library binding : alk. paper) --
ISBN 978-1-4271-9558-6 (electronic (pdf))
1. Hudgens, Vanessa, 1988- ---Juvenile literature. 2. Actors--United States--Biography--Juvenile literature. 3. Singers--United States--Biography--Juvenile literature. I. Title.
PN2287.H737S54 2010
791.4302'8092--dc22
[B]
                                            2010032494

Crabtree Publishing Company
www.crabtreebooks.com   1-800-387-7650

Printed in the USA/102010/SP20100915

Published in Canada
Crabtree Publishing
616 Welland Ave.
St. Catharines, ON
L2M 5V6

Published in the United States
Crabtree Publishing
PMB 59051
350 Fifth Avenue, 59th Floor
New York, New York 10118

Published in the United Kingdom
Crabtree Publishing
Maritime House
Basin Road North, Hove
BN41 1WR

Published in Australia
Crabtree Publishing
386 Mt. Alexander Rd.
Ascot Vale (Melbourne)
VIC 3032

CONTENTS

Words that are defined in the glossary are in
bold type the first time they appear in the text.

The Rest Is Herstory

When Vanessa Hudgens stepped onto the stage to try out for a lead role in Disney's *High School Musical*, she was one of more than 600 hopefuls. At that time, she was not well known. In fact, Vanessa had only a few minor parts to her credit. When she **auditioned**, however—singing the Jessica Simpson song "Angels"—she blew the producers away. Vanessa was chosen for the leading part of Gabriella Montez. The role put the young singer/actress on the path to stardom.

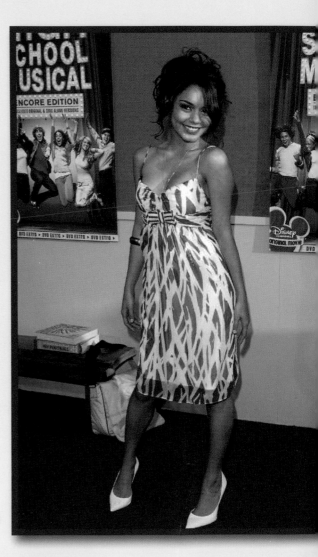

Tough Competition

Vanessa had some tough competition when she tried out for *High School Musical*. She beat out Diana DeGarmo, who was the runner-up during the third season of the popular TV show *American Idol*.

Meet Vanessa

Vanessa's work in *High School Musical* and the two **sequels** to the film have made her extremely popular with young fans. She has won awards for her work as both an actress and a singer. In addition to being featured on the soundtrack albums from her movies, Vanessa has released two solo CDs. Critics and fans alike call her a "triple threat" because she acts, sings, and dances.

It's not surprising that music is such an important part of Vanessa's career. When she was a little girl, Vanessa took piano lessons, dance classes, and voice lessons. In addition, her family has a musical history. Both sets of Vanessa's grandparents were band musicians during the **Big Band** era, which took place during the 1930s and 1940s.

More Than Meets the Eye

In addition to her talent, Vanessa is known for her **exotic** beauty. She is 5'3" (160 cm) tall, with dark hair that **cascades** around her heart-shaped face. Her brown eyes sparkle and light up when she smiles. Her natural beauty and friendly manner, however, are only part of Vanessa's charm. Her inner beauty also shines through in the volunteer work she does.

Preschool Star

Vanessa's very first acting role was in a pre-school Christmas play when she was only three years old. She hadn't told her parents about it, so they were quite surprised to see Vanessa on stage as Mary, singing "Away in a Manger."

Paparazzi try to get pictures of Vanessa out shopping with a friend.

She Said It

"Paparazzi are a nuisance because it doesn't have anything to do with your actual job, which for me is acting and movies. Instead, they take interest in me filling up my tank at the gas station and random things. I think it's unnecessary but it's something that comes with the territory."

—On the downside of fame, interview in *Newsweek* magazine, September 2009

Guitar Heroine

Vanessa recently learned to play the guitar. She used her new guitar skills while performing the song "Everything I Own" in the 2009 movie *Bandslam*. Vanessa says she thinks it would also be fun to learn to play the drums.

Vanessa plays the guitar in a scene from *Bandslam*.

Rising Star

Vanessa Hudgens became a star almost instantly with the success of *High School Musical*. What may have seemed like "overnight success," however, was actually the result of nearly a **decade** of hard work. Years of dance classes, voice and music lessons, auditions, bit parts, and determination all came before Vanessa skyrocketed to fame.

MULTICULTURAL

Vanessa's family has a rich **ethnic** background. Her mother was born in the Philippines and is part Filipino, Chinese, and Spanish. Her father is part Irish and part Native American.

Vanessa with her father

A Star Is Born

Vanessa Anne Hudgens was born on December 14, 1988, in Salinas, California. She spent her early years in this small city, which is located between San Francisco and Los Angeles on the California coast. Then her family began a series of moves, spending time in Oregon and Southern California. As Vanessa's career began to develop, the family decided to settle in Los Angeles so Vanessa could continue to pursue her dreams of singing and acting.

Family Matters

Vanessa's parents worked hard when she was growing up. Her father Greg Hudgens worked as a firefighter, and her mother Gina Guangco worked at different office jobs. Vanessa is close to her family, which includes her sister Stella who is seven years younger than her.

Vanessa (left) with her sister (middle) and her mom (right)

Vanessa gets her cheery nature from her mother.

She Said It

"*I love her to death. She's the sweetest, happiest woman I've ever met, the most free-spirited, delightful person, and I* **aspire** *to be just like her. The older I get, the more I find myself like my mom. She just has the best outlook.*"
—Talking about her mother in *Allure* magazine, October 2009

In Her Sister's Footsteps

Stella Hudgens is also an actress. She has appeared in commercials and had minor roles in television series such as *American Family*, *Single with Parents*, and *Deeply Irresponsible*. Stella also appeared in the 2007 movie *The Memory Thief*.

Stella Hudgens

School Days

Vanessa attended various schools when she was growing up. She left school after she finished the seventh grade at Orange County High School of the Arts in Santa Ana, California. Her mother then **homeschooled** both Vanessa and Stella. Vanessa later "experienced" high school—even going to the prom—when she appeared in *High School Musical*.

Taking the Stage

Vanessa's acting career began when she was eight years old. She played the part of a munchkin in a community theater production of *The Wizard of Oz*. Over the next two years, Vanessa appeared in other local theater productions, such as *Evita, Carousel, The King and I, The Music Man, Cinderella,* and *Damn Yankees*. She also played the part of Cindy Lou in a production of *How the Grinch Stole Christmas*.

Vanessa Hudgens had a starring role in the movie *Thunderbirds*.

Vanessa's career took a new turn when she did a favor for a friend. The friend was auditioning for a part in a commercial, and she asked Vanessa to go with her. Vanessa got the part! At that point, her career began to take off. "One thing just led to another," she said. "I did a commercial and then another one. I started getting guest spots on TV shows and went on from there."

—Interview for Inquirer.net, August 9, 2007

Showing Up!

When she was 13, Vanessa moved on to television and film roles. In 2002, she appeared in episodes of the television shows *Still Standing* and *Robbery Homicide Division*. Over the next few years, she appeared in the shows *Quintuplets* and *The Brothers García*. She also

landed small parts in the dramatic movies *Thirteen* (2003) and the science-fiction movie *Thunderbirds* (2004) before landing her breakout role in *High School Musical*.

LIMITED TALENT?

You would never guess it from all the professional dancing she has done, but Vanessa admits to sometimes being somewhat clumsy. She says she has even fallen down stairs! In addition, Vanessa has never been able to whistle!

Teen TV

High School Musical was not Vanessa's only work for the Disney Channel. In addition to her work in *HSM*, she played a character named Corrie in four episodes of *The Suite Life of Zack and Cody* in 2006. The same year, she also appeared in two episodes of *Drake & Josh* on Nickelodeon.

The Stages of Her Life

Vanessa's different talents have led to her success as both an actress and a singer. No doubt she had dreamed of that one big role—the part that would help her career skyrocket. Even so, it's unlikely that she, or any of the young actors cast in *High School Musical*, ever imagined just how huge it would become.

High School Musical

The made-for-TV movie *High School Musical* **premiered** on January 20, 2006. It became the most successful movie the Disney Channel ever produced.

In *HSM*, Vanessa plays the brainy, shy, and beautiful Gabriella Montez who forms an unlikely friendship with Troy Bolton (played by Zac Efron), the star of East High School's basketball team. Troy and Gabriella surprise everyone when they team up to audition for the upcoming school musical. At least one other student, Sharpay Evans (played by Ashley Tisdale), is unhappy about the situation. She wants the lead—and Troy—for herself, and she employs several dirty tricks to try to ruin Gabriella's chances. Fortunately, other students work together to make sure Troy and Gabriella don't miss the chance to follow their dreams.

Throughout the drama, the audience is treated to a series of catchy songs that create the backdrop for some high-energy dance numbers. While several songs from the movie's soundtrack ranked high on the charts, "Breaking Free" proved to be the biggest hit. The song made it onto top ten lists at home and around the world.

She Said It

"She's kind of the brainy girl who just likes to cuddle up with a good book. I like playing the role because it's nice to show that the brainy girls can also be pretty. Usually when brainy girls are shown in films, they kind of are presented as nerds or someone not very social."

–on her role as Gabriella Montez, in *All in This Together: The Unofficial Story of High School Musical* (2007)

Vanessa (right) poses with fellow cast members from *High School Musical*.

High on the Charts

High School Musical was the Disney Channel's most watched movie of 2006, with 7.7 million viewers tuning in to the premiere broadcast in the United States. It has now been seen by more than 255 million viewers around the world. In addition to its success on television, the *HSM* soundtrack was the best-selling album in the United States in 2006, with sales of nearly four million copies.

High School Musical 2

The tremendous success of *High School Musical* led Disney to make a sequel. *High School Musical 2*—also a made-for-television movie—**debuted** on the Disney Channel on August 17, 2007. More than 18 million viewers in the United States watched the premiere—almost 6 million more than the number who watched the premiere of the original *HSM*. This made *HSM 2* the highest-rated Disney Channel movie of all time and the number one cable telecast of all time.

All of the lead actors returned for the sequel, which is set during summer vacation. Gabriella, Troy, and several other East High students have landed great summer jobs at a country club. The friends are excited to be working at the club, but there's a problem. Sharpay's father owns the club, and she has only one thing on her mind—to lure Troy away from Gabriella. When it seems that Sharpay's plan is working, Gabriella quits her job at the club, breaks up with Troy, and leaves. Troy's heart is broken, but when Gabriella shows up to perform in the club's talent show, the two make up and share their first romantic kiss.

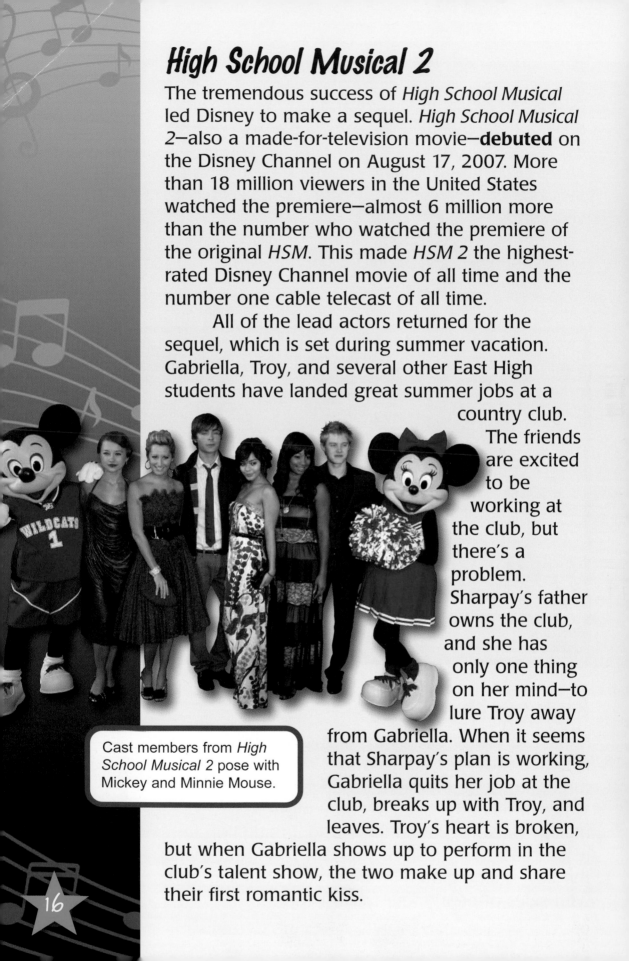

Cast members from *High School Musical 2* pose with Mickey and Minnie Mouse.

High School Musical 3: Senior Year

After the huge success of the made-for-TV movies, Disney decided to make *High School Musical 3: Senior Year* for the big screen. It was released in theaters in October 2008. In the film, Gabriella and her friends are now seniors, and they are facing some big choices. Gabriella and Troy know that their paths are about to take them in different directions. They organize a musical about their lives and futures. Gabriella decides to leave East High early to attend college, but she and Troy are reunited in the end. Meanwhile, their friends make important decisions about their own futures.

NEXT GENERATION

Now that their characters have graduated, Vanessa and some of the other stars of the first three *HSM* films will no longer be featured in future productions. New characters will be introduced in the next made-for-television movie called *High School Musical 4: East Meets West*.

Vanessa (below left) dances up a storm in *High School Musical 3: Senior Year*.

V for Victory

In the middle of making the *HSM* movies, Vanessa began a recording career. Her debut solo album was released by Hollywood Records in September 2006. According to Vanessa, the title of the album—*V*—stands for "Vanessa" and "variety." *V* is a cool combination of pop, rock, dance, and electronic music. The album debuted at number 24 on the Billboard 200 Chart and sold 34,000 copies the very first week. *V* was later certified gold in the United States, which means it sold more than half a million copies. The first single released from *V* was "Come Back to Me." The song rose to number 28 on the Billboard pop chart.

The Concert Scene

To help **promote** *V*, Vanessa hit the stage in 15 cities in the fall of 2006. She and Jordan Pruitt were the opening acts for the Cheetah Girls' The Party's Just Begun Tour. Before she went on tour herself, Vanessa had never been to a concert! Soon after the Cheetah Girls' tour, Vanessa and most of her *HSM* co-stars began a 40-city concert tour in the United States, Canada, Mexico, and South America.

> The *High School Musical* co-stars began a 40-city concert tour in 2006.

She Said It

"Touring is tough. You're almost in a haze because you don't really know where you are half the time: You're in a hotel room one moment, and the next thing you know, you're onstage performing for 60,000 people, then you're back on an airplane. It's very hectic and I couldn't do it without my family."
—In an interview in *Teen* magazine, September 2007

Identified

Vanessa's second CD *Identified* was released in July 2008. This CD showcases richer vocals and a more mature sound than *V*. In *Identified*, Vanessa seems to have found her comfort zone with pounding dance tracks that come together with a funkier, jazzed-up sound. *Identified* debuted at number 23 on the Billboard 200 charts and sold 22,000 copies the first week. "Sneakernight" was the only single released from the album, which Vanessa promoted with a tour of 19 state fairs in August and September 2008. Vanessa was the headliner of the tour, with opening acts from Corbin Bleu (her *High School Musical* co-star), Jordan Pruitt, Drew Seeley, and Mandy Moore.

Vanessa performs a song on her 2008 *Identified* tour.

She Said It

"When you're acting, you're a character and you can hide behind that. Music is who you are right then and there—you can't hide. Right now, I don't know completely who I am, but I'm comfortable in my own skin."
—In an interview in *CosmoGirl*, August 2008

Getting Noticed

Vanessa's beauty and style have not gone unnoticed by fashion judges. For example, *Teen Vogue* has included her on its monthly Ten Best Dressed lists. She was ranked number 10 in *Cosmopolitan* magazine's list of Best Dressed Celebs of 2008. She was also included in *People* magazine's 100 Most Beautiful People lists in both 2008 and 2009.

IN THE SPOTLIGHT

Not all publicity is good. In 2007 and again in 2009, some private and revealing photos of her were made public. Vanessa was very embarrassed. She apologized to her fans because she said their support and trust means the world to her.

Surprisingly Private

Vanessa is surprisingly private for a famous person. She once told reporters, "I like to keep my personal life to myself, so people almost invading it is odd, but I respect the fans. They just want to know more." When Vanessa was a guest on *Ellen* Ellen DeGeneres teased Vanessa about not revealing more about her private life. Ellen said, "I have more questions about important things…that you won't answer."

High School Graduate

Today, Vanessa continues to move forward in her acting career, taking on new challenges and roles. She has already made her mark in the film and music industries. New movie roles have given her the chance to show how **versatile** she is as an actress. In addition to developing her professional life, Vanessa has flourished in her personal life, which is now filled with friendships, romance, charities, and greater independence.

Bandslam

Vanessa took on a very different role in the romantic comedy *Bandslam*. Vanessa plays Sa5m (the 5 is silent)—an offbeat, **introverted**, and **deadpan** girl. She and a newcomer to the school named Will Burton (played by Gaelan Connell) are considered social misfits. Both are surprised when they end up in a band with super-popular Charlotte (played by Aly Michalka) to compete in an annual school contest. A terrible discovery threatens their chances right before the competition.

Bandslam was released on August 14, 2009. Reviews were largely favorable for this entertaining combination of music and teen drama.

Another Side to Vanessa

Vanessa showed her fun side doing the voices for several characters on an episode of *Robot Chicken*, which first aired in September 2009. *Robot Chicken* is a stop-motion animated TV series that pokes fun at pop culture. It airs on the Cartoon Network's Adult Swim block of programs, which are geared toward older teens and adults.

Vanessa tries to transform hideous monster Alex Pettyfer back into his former self in *Beastly*.

Beastly

Vanessa's next movie *Beastly* is a modern-day beauty-and-the-beast story. She co-starred with British actor Alex Pettyfer, who plays the role of Kyle Kingson—a handsome rich kid who is **transformed** into a **hideous** monster after he ditches a date (played by Mary-Kate Olsen). The curse can only be broken if he finds true love. Enter Vanessa's character Linda Taylor. Vanessa says Linda is not the typical "beauty" **portrayed** in such films. She describes her role as a young woman who is artistic, free-spirited, strong, and independent. *Beastly* is scheduled to hit theaters in March 2011.

Sucker Punch

Vanessa moved on to another big-screen project with a more adult role as Blondie in the action film *Sucker Punch*. Director Zack Snyder described *Sucker Punch* as a kind of "Alice in Wonderland with machine guns."

In the movie, a young woman called Baby Doll (played by Emily Browning) is sent to a mental health facility by her evil stepfather, who plans to have her undergo a brain operation called a **lobotomy**. While there, she deals with her situation by imagining a different reality, one that allows her to escape. Vanessa plays the supporting role of Blondie, a fellow patient who befriends the troubled girl. *Sucker Punch* is scheduled to be released in March 2011.

The cast of *Sucker Punch* poses together. Music and dancing transports the movie's characters to fantasy worlds.

And the Winner Is...

Vanessa has won three Teen Choice Awards! One was for TV Chemistry (2006), shared with Zac Efron for *High School Musical*. The others were for Female Music Breakout Artist (2007) and Female Hottie (2008). In 2009, Vanessa also won a Nickelodeon Kids' Choice Award for Favorite Female Movie Actress. In 2010, she took home the award for Female Star of Tomorrow at the ShoWest 2010 Final Night Awards.

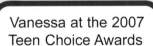
Vanessa at the 2007 Teen Choice Awards

Paying the Rent

In August 2010, Vanessa went back to the stage. She starred in a production of the musical *RENT* at the Hollywood Bowl in California. Made famous on Broadway in the 1990s, *RENT* is a rock opera about a group of struggling young artists and musicians. Vanessa starred as Mimi, the drug-addicted dancer who is battling AIDS. In an interview with JustJaredJr.com in July, she said, "I'm just excited to get up on that stage again. It's been like a decade I think…I'm so long overdue."

25

On the Personal Side

Vanessa has been dating Zac Efron since they met while filming *High School Musical*. The two are very private about their relationship, but sometimes actions speak louder than words. For example, Zac threw a surprise 21st birthday party in 2009 for Vanessa and 100 of her friends at a Hollywood restaurant. He also had orange, lemon, and tangerine trees planted in her yard.

The pair often refuse to discuss each other or their relationship in public. But in an appearance on *Ellen*, Vanessa did give in enough to giggle and make a thumbs-up sign when asked if Zac was a good kisser.

Vanessa and boyfriend Zac Efron looked picture perfect together at the 81st Academy Awards.

Academy Award Appearance

In February 2009, Vanessa and Zac joined Hugh Jackman, Beyoncé, and other stars in a song and dance number at the 81st Academy Awards. The group performed a **medley** of songs featured in both old and new musicals. It was a celebration of the renewed popularity of the musical.

Vanessa makes friends easily and has formed close relationships with some of the girls she has worked with. She is friends with actresses Ashley Tisdale, Aly Michalka, Brittany Snow, Samantha Droke, and Nikki Reed, as well as with her *High School Musical* co-star Corbin Bleu.

Home Alone

Vanessa bought a home of her own in Studio City, California, in 2008. The house has six bedrooms, six bathrooms, and three fireplaces, and cost $2.75 million! But Vanessa is well paid for her work. In December 2008, she was listed at number 20 on *Forbes* magazine's list of High Earners Under 30.

Vanessa Hudgens's home

A Helping Hand

Vanessa finds time in her busy schedule to do volunteer work for some of her favorite charities. They include Best Buddies International (an organization that helps people with mental disabilities), St. Jude Children's Research Hospital, Lollipop Theater Network (an organization that arranges showings of first-run movies for children in hospitals), and VH1 Save The Music Foundation (which promotes music education in schools). In addition, Vanessa sang the song "Winter Wonderland" on the album *A Very Special Christmas 7*, which benefitted the Special Olympics. The album was released in late 2009.

Vanessa helped promote the Stand Up to Cancer program by attending the one-hour telethon on September 10, 2010.

Shine On, Vanessa!

From humble beginnings in community theater, all the way to big-screen movie star, Vanessa Hudgens has shown how talent and hard work can make dreams come true. The young singer/actress has every reason to expect that her star will continue to rise and her fans can look forward to enjoying Vanessa's talents in the years ahead.

Timeline

1988: Vanessa Anne Hudgens is born in Salinas, California, on December 14.

1996: Begins performing in community theater

2002: She lands roles in the television shows *Still Standing* and *Robbery Homicide Division*.

2003: Appears in the film *Thirteen* and the television show *The Brothers Garcia*.

2004: Appears in the film *Thunderbirds*.

2006: The smash Disney made-for-television movie *High School Musical* debuts in January, with Vanessa starring as Gabriella Montez.

2006: Appears in the TV shows *Drake & Josh* and *The Suite Life of Zack and Cody*.

2006: Her first solo CD *V* is released, and she goes on tour to promote it.

2007: *High School Musical 2* appears on television in August, with Vanessa again in her role as Gabriella Montez.

2008: *High School Musical 3: Senior Year* premieres in theaters in October, with Vanessa again playing Gabriella Montez.

2008: Her second CD *Identified* is released, and she goes on tour to promote it.

2009: The romantic comedy film *Bandslam* is released in August, with Vanessa playing the role of Sa5m.

2010: Stars on stage in the rock opera *RENT*, at the Hollywood Bowl in California in August.

2011: The fantasy romance film *Beastly* is scheduled to be released in March, with Vanessa playing the role of Linda Taylor.

2011: The action-fantasy film *Sucker Punch* is scheduled to be released in March, with Vanessa playing the role of Blondie.

Glossary

aspire To aim for or try to accomplish a goal

auditioned Performed a short scene to try out for a part

Big Band A type of music involving large dance or jazz bands that became popular during the 1930s and 1940s

cascade To spill or flow downward, like a waterfall

deadpan Without expression, showing no emotion

debuted Performed for the first time

decade A period of time spanning 10 years

ethnic Having to do with a group of people who share the same national origin, language, or culture

exotic Interesting and unusual, often foreign

hideous Shockingly ugly; gruesome looking

homeschooled Taught someone their school lessons at home

introverted Shy and reserved, keeping one's feelings and thoughts private

lobotomy An operation removing part of the brain to control a person's behavior

medley A song created from parts of many songs

paparazzi Photographers who follow famous people around to take pictures of them

portrayed Revealed, showed, or described in a visual way

premiere The first public performance of a movie, show, or work of music

promote To share information to create interest in a product

sequels Books or movies that continue the story told in a previous book or movie

transformed Altered or changed greatly

versatile Talented or useful in many different ways

Find Out More

Books

Boone, Mary. *Vanessa Anne Hudgens*. Hockessin, DE: Mitchell Lane Publishers, 2009.

Mooney, Carla. *Vanessa Hudgens*. Broomall, PA: Mason Crest Publishers, 2009.

Norwich, Grace. *Vanessa Hudgens: Breaking Free: An Unauthorized Biography*. New York: Price Stern Sloan, 2007.

Rawson, Katherine. *Vanessa Hudgens*. New York: PowerKids Press, 2010.

Tieck, Sarah. *Vanessa Hudgens*. Edina, MA: Buddy Books, 2008.

Websites

Vanessa Hudgens on MySpace
  www.myspace.com/vanessahudgens

Fan sites
  http://vanessa-anne.org/
  http://vanessaanneonline.net/

High School Musical sites

High School Musical
  http://tv.disney.go.com/disneychannel/original movies/highschoolmusical/index.html

High School Musical 2
  http://tv.disney.go.com/disneychannel/original movies/highschoolmusical2/

High School Musical 3: Senior Year
  http://adisney.go.com/disneyvideos/television/ highschoolmusical/

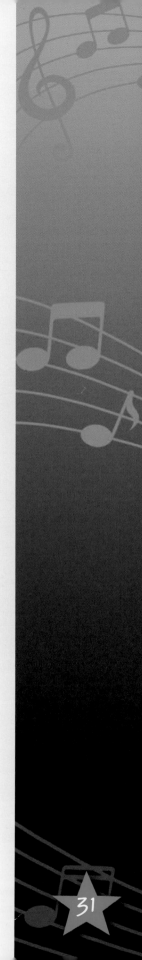

Index

About the Author

Writing for young people comes naturally to Valerie Sherrard, a former group-home director and foster parent to approximately 70 teenagers. Sherrard's books have been shortlisted for numerous awards. Valerie blogs infrequently at:
http://valeriesherrard.blogspot.com